Survive and Thrive in High School:
From One High Schooler to Another

Emaleigh Mowry

Emaleigh Mowry
#Survive & Thrive

Copyright © 2016 Emaleigh Mowry

ISBN: 978-0-9976987-0-1

Images and cover designed by Cole Fungaroli

Book Dedication

To Jacob and Cole… For all the days you took care of me in high school, and for teaching me what it means to have some fun. Good luck over the next few years of your schoolings. I have a feeling both of you will do well.

And to my incredibly supportive family who have always and will continue to push me to do my best.

Table of Contents

Decisions, Decisions 1
Positive Goals 9
Routine 23
Organize and Prioritize 35
Relationships 45
Failure and Confidence.....55

Survive and Thrive in High School:
From One High Schooler to Another

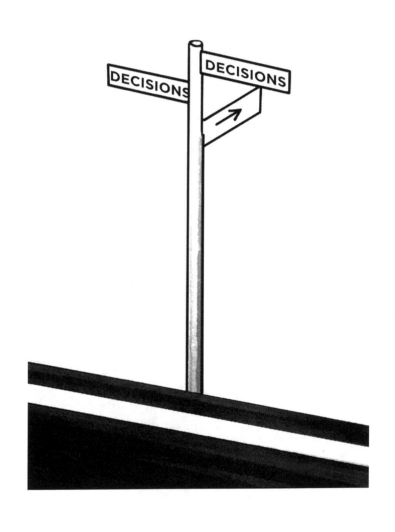

Decisions, Decisions

"It's not hard to make decisions when you know what your values are." ~ Roy Disney

I once had to write a speech for a public speaking competition. I wanted to have a memorable ending, so with the help of my advisor, we came up with this: "A pessimist complains about the wind, the optimist expects it to change, and the realist adjusts the sail."

I have decided to be a realist, and thanks to some events in my past, I have a better understanding of the life that I want to live. I knew that I was not going to complain about things I could not change because that brought me down, and I definitely was not going to sit around and wait for it to get better. I had ultimately decided to be in control of my sail (or life in this case). This is the first lesson I hope to share with you.

At a young age, I decided that I *had* to take responsibility for myself. I ended up doing everything that I could to create an impressive life that others could admire. I had role models to look up to from a distance, but I was really looking for someone close that I could relate with. I think I shaped my life to be an image of what I would expect my ideal role model to look and act like. I then saw the potential that I had within myself and did not want to let it all go to waste... I have watched one too many other people in my life do that, and you better bet that I was not going to let myself go down that same path.

I strived to be a beacon for others, not just an image, but an actual role model, and I realized that once I did something well or admirable, others took notice. When this happened, there was a newfound sense of pride and satisfaction instilled within me. This book is my way of laying out my game plan for life, particularly life in high school. I want to share my success with you readers and help you live your best possible life. I want you to feel that overwhelming sense of pride and accomplishment as well.

I have surrounded myself with supportive individuals because it is so much easier for me to be around positive people rather than negative ones. If I had the power, I would get rid of all the pessimistic people in my life. Unfortunately, I'm stuck with some, but it has made me appreciate my outlook all the more. When I watch people make bad choices around me, I'm able to learn more about how I want to live my life. I don't let their bad decisions influence me in a negative way. Inversely, I let them have a positive impact. This book is just one of the positive impacts that have resulted.

I am writing this book as I prepare to wrap up my last year of high school, having now have a much better understanding of what I want and don't want. These past four years have been the most impactful and meaningful for me personally, and I have noticed the same to be true for my peers as well. So cheers from me to you for deciding to take the first step towards living your best life.

One lesson that I have quickly learned in my lifetime is that *you* ultimately control what happens in *your* life. *You* make the final decisions, and others cannot make these for you. How important it is to realize that those you make today will dictate the life you live tomorrow. Being in control of your life is a decision that you have to make for

> One lesson that I have quickly learned in my lifetime is that *you* ultimately control what happens in *your* life.

yourself so that you can determine what kind of life you really want to be living.

We have been given the gift of choice for a reason. It has been left up to us to decide what kinds of choices we will make in life, but as human beings, we make both good and bad ones.

Making mistakes is inevitable. It's a part of life that we should start to appreciate. If we did not fail or go through some challenges, how would we ever learn? Some of the best life lessons will come from your failures. On the bright side, they will also happen to be some of the best stories to tell when you grow older.

Look for a lesson in all that you're involved in. Ten times out of ten there will be something, no matter how big or small, that you can take from every situation. Sometimes it's easier to understand what you don't want rather than what you do. High school is the perfect time to discover and make something out of ourselves.

Now is the time to be a realist. After high school, no one wants to be forgotten. We want to be remembered as extraordinary individuals. So just keep this thought in the back of your mind while you journey through your high school career- you are the boss of your life. You make the final decisions, so it's time to start making the right ones.

I am encouraging you to adjust your sail and get control of your life. No one else is going to do this for you.

Fast Action Step:

Post a selfie on your social media with the hashtag #SurviveAndThrive to announce your dedication to this important decision to control your life. Search the hashtag to see who else is a part of the movement and encourage their journey.

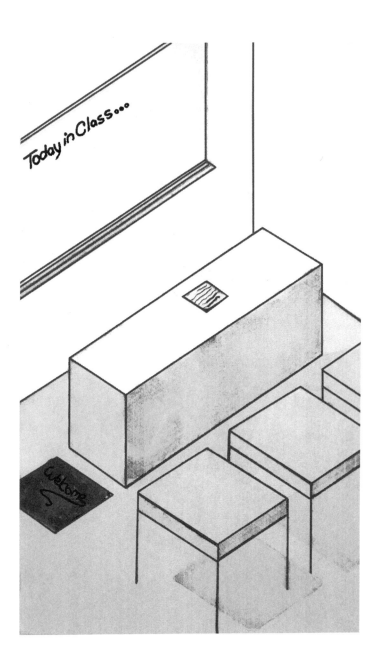

Positive Goals

"How am I going to live today in order to create the tomorrow I'm committed to?" ~ Anthony Robbins

This next lesson is about choosing the kind of mindset that you want to live with. I believe that living with a positive mindset gives you the best results. I have laced my life with positivity, and by doing this, I have learned to set beneficial goals for myself. They give me something to go after and work hard for. Once I reach a goal, I feel that self-pride all over again. It makes me feel worth something special. I am here to help you find that same mindset so you can live up to your maximum potential.

The first way to do this is to set goals for yourself. There are five major categories where it's necessary to define your goals: personal, school, clubs and activities, family and friends, and college. If you incorporate goals within these areas of your life, you will most definitely be ready to go out and succeed in no time.

The first category is personal. As I said a little earlier, it's very important that you work on yourself before you do anything else. Set personal goals because they will make you a better person, and that will allow all of the other areas of your life to fall into place.

Failure to execute and making excuses are your biggest roadblocks when aiming to achieve your personal goals. In high school, we struggle and worry about what others think of us rather than focusing on what we think of ourselves. We push our wants, needs, and goals to the back burner. Make yourself your number one priority and put yourself first. Don't worry too much about what others expect of you; it's all about what you expect of yourself. That's where the great personal goals stem from.

Setting goals for your high school career is essential. High school is truly all about learning how to create effective study habits and work ethic. This is the time for you to start preparing for your future. Life will be much less complicated for you down the road once you've implemented those efficient work and study habits.

It's very easy to pick out students who are slacking in those areas because their bad habits become evident through their transcripts. Thinking about eventually heading to college or getting a job some day? Admissions offices for colleges and future employers will take a hard look at your high school transcript, checking up on your dependability, efficiency, and organization. Make sure your records reflect your good habits.

Personally, I have struggled with maintaining above-average grades in my classes. Now I am not saying that I don't earn those grades, I'm just saying that I have had to work extremely hard to do so well in the classroom. I give all of the credit to the study habits that I have instilled in my life. They make it so much easier to stay organized, be responsible in class, and definitely take some of the stress away.

Good classroom habits will also make the transition from high school to college so much easier. Once you have a solid foundation, you will know how to be prepared. Taking upper level courses or even just classes that challenge you are what creates a sense of preparedness. I know that I feel prepared for lots of things that life has to throw at me because I have equipped myself for my future success by giving myself the tools necessary to be successful.

Unfortunately, today, it can be so tempting to close our books, toss our notes to the side, and grab for our cell phones. Students fail because they're lazy and don't want to take control of the situation. But once again, this is *your* life, and implementing the necessary amount of self-discipline is something you need to do for yourself. Start to focus on what needs to be done in order to go after the goals you set for your grades.

Being goal-oriented while involved with different organizations and clubs can allow you to really get the most out of your personal investments outside of the classroom. Typically, we only join certain teams because we are interested in them. We are more willing to give up our time to the extra things that we believe count. These are what give our lives some substance and make us feel more complete. We find these activities to be rewarding and favorable, which makes it all the easier to set goals and thrive in this area- reaping the rewards long after high school!

Sadly, some kids lack determination and fail to take full advantage of the opportunities that their activities have to offer. It may get difficult trying to balance all of the hard classes that you're taking and the clubs that want all of your precious time. But fear not and do not let it overwhelm you. For now, give yourself the mindset that you will do your absolute best in your clubs, and then let the benefits start to roll in.

From my personal experience, I have learned that the best place to find information about school clubs is the upperclassmen. They have already been through everything and undoubtedly know the ins and outs of every activity. They have the stories to tell that you need to hear. Don't be afraid to approach them because most older kids will be more than glad to help you with your questions and offer advice. After all, their high school years are almost over, so let them share their experiences. Many are sad to be leaving high school and would probably have that "self-worth" feeling by being approached for advice from an underclassman. Another idea is to ask a class officer or a student council member to help assist you in finding the right activity.

When it comes to friends in high school, I like to stick with a saying that my parents frequently quoted to me, "you are who you run with." It makes complete sense. Whatever the attitudes and behaviors of those you spend most of your time with could be reflected in you. Begin to watch how you act around your friends. It is easy to pick up good and/or bad traits from others and soon they can start being your own too.

Set goals with your friends because you will become a reflection of those with whom you spend the most time. You must choose the right group of friends who have similar goals and values so that their influence adds to you and doesn't take away from you. That way you can stay successful in high school and really have an overall great time. With some good friends to rely on and relax with, you will be making great memories. I have found that with a close group of true friends, you can divide and conquer and accomplish so much more. The more the merrier when it comes to accomplishing great things.

Having a positive friend group will really make you more productive, and you will tend to be more successful when achieving your goals. However, high school is the time when people change and show their true colors. This was a big eye opener for me. I am so glad that I changed my friend group for the better since my freshman year. I realized the people who hung around me were big competitors and not in a good way. They stressed me out and often brought me down. I quickly assessed what I wanted and needed in my friend group, and made the necessary changes. Since then, I have had nothing but an overwhelming abundance of support and love from my friends.

Whether a majority of your time is spent with the basketball team or the chess club, it's imperative that you surround yourself with people who are willing to support you and help to keep you on track throughout school and life. If you're finding that some friends

> People change and so will you.

that you have been long-time bff's with aren't following along the same path that you are, it's time to do some trimming. Be willing and prepared to tailor your friend group to include the people who will support and encourage you the most. People change and so will you. Make the necessary changes when needed so that you can be as constructive as possible.

The next big step after high school is usually college. Often, people are afraid of the college commitment because they wait until late in their high school years to decide what they want to do and where they want to go. It's really important that we set goals for college throughout our entire high school career so it's not as overwhelming.

When it came to college, I had *no* idea where to start. I am the oldest child in my family, and my parents had very little college experience. I felt like I was playing pin the tail on the college while blindfolded. I was fortunate enough to have the help of a close family friend.

College isn't for everyone. And that's okay. But for those of you who want to go to college, you *need* to be informed and prepared to go down that road.

College costs a pretty penny, but if you take it seriously, you will earn your pretty pennies back and then some. Don't wait until your senior year. Sometimes that's too late, and you could lose precious opportunities and scholarships!

If you're proactive and start things your freshman year, I promise it will be so much simpler, and you'll have more time to think things through and take one step at a time. Start setting goals oriented around college for each year of high school. Break down the process, understand things, and really feel it out. The beauty of this process is that you give yourself plenty of time to ask questions and get help if needed. You can achieve your college goals by being informed and prepared. Make a schedule for freshman, sophomore, junior, and senior year that includes what you plan on getting done for that year and edit as you go.

If you follow that process, it will really make applying and deciding so much faster and stress free. You first need to have an idea of what you want to do with your life. Then, research some colleges that fit your criteria. That will help you out in the long-run.

It's easy to see that setting goals for your life can be extremely rewarding. When you begin to set goals for yourself, you are simultaneously choosing to have a positive mindset. Your goals are something to strive for and achieve. It will be exciting for those around you to see what you go out and accomplish.

Fast Action Step:

Post a picture of yourself in the "power pose" with the hashtag #SurviveAndThrive to announce your dedication to this important decision to control your life. Search the hashtag to see who else is a part of the movement and encourage their journey.

Routine

"Nothing will work unless you do." ~ Maya Angelou

Routine has been a major part of my life, and I contribute a significant amount of my success to the routines that I have ingrained in my life.

My senior year of high school was much different than the previous ones. By my junior year I had it all figured out, and my routine was working just fine for me. I was being productive and reaching my daily goals; however, when my senior year came around, my life and my beloved routine were kind of tossed tipsy-turvy. I only had three classes at school scheduled, and they were all right smack dab in the middle of the day. I hated it because I am a morning person, and at first felt as though I was wasting my mornings. What was I supposed to do until 10:00 am?

Finally, I had found my solutions. With the help of trial and error (trust me I tried a different thing every day just finding out what I liked and wanted to incorporate into my schedule), I figured out that I didn't have to waste my mornings. I decided that it would be best for me just to get up and go to the gym to work out as soon as I got up so I could start my day off being super productive! So, I went to the gym, got ready for the day, went to school, went home to do chores, homework, and then had the evenings to hang out with my family and friends.

Eventually I learned to love my new routine. It really allowed me to balance my social, academic, and personal life, and I even had room to squeeze in things that weren't planned way ahead of time. My time spent this way allowed me to learn a lot about myself which I enjoyed, and it was due to my senior year game plan. A lot of my close friends had the same class schedule as me, so it worked out quite well. I could balance basically everything in my life, and I could enjoy my days after I had found my plan rather than hate my senior year schedule because I didn't have a likable routine.

Routines are important because they're basically a game plan for your life. When it comes to game plans, aren't they usually used by people aiming for set goals? Sports teams, politicians, and teachers use game plans for practically everything. They know how to win and succeed because of their plans, so it just seems fitting that the same could be true for each of us if we propose a "game plan" of our own for our daily life?

Your game plan should simplify your life. It should make it easier for you to get more things done in a shorter period of time. Scattered, less strict routines can make your life seem more disorganized than before. With a sound routine, you are more focused. You are tuned into the task at hand and less likely to fall for distractions.

Create a schedule for your weekdays and weekends. Maybe on the weekdays you will get up early before school like I did and go to the gym. Then you will head to school, go to any extracurricular activities that you're involved in, go home for dinner, do some homework, then relax and do something fun for yourself. Then on the weekends you can sleep in, do little odds and ends that you didn't get to finish throughout the week, then hang out with your friends, and just have a good time. If you make up a game plan something like that, your days will be preset, and you will relieve yourself of some unnecessary stress.

Routines also create structure in your life. They get your life in order. This structure alleviates you from always having to make decisions. You can wake up every day feeling as if you have a sense of purpose and organization. Everyone loves being organized, even if you aren't all that put together all the time.

So brush the dirt off your knees; it's time to shape up your life! I promise you that you will thank yourself over and over again once you implement a well-balanced routine into your life. You'll want to pinch yourself for not starting this sooner!

It's very important to find a routine that works for you and stick with it. You will get a lot more bang for your buck once you've found a good rhythm. With good routine comes good habit, and good habit is a wonderful thing.

Routine is a healthy habit, and in life, one good habit will inevitably lead to another. This will cause you to want to make better decisions for yourself, so in the end you keep building up all of these positive things in your life.

The key here is to do things every day that you enjoy. As long as you do things that you feel good about doing, you will live a happy and healthy life. You will begin to look forward to the next Monday rather than dread it. You run the routines; the routines don't run you.

Follow through with your game plan, and you will be set. You won't need to be constantly worrying about what you will be doing each day because you will be unconsciously going through the things on your schedule.

Again, you will thank yourself for implementing a daily routine in your life. It saves you so much time, effort, and work. You will see a noticeable difference in the way you conduct your life once a routine is in place.

It is also important to know that if you find, after a few days, that your original plan isn't working out the way you thought it would, it is completely OK for you to change it. That is the whole point of creating a routine! Routines are intended to make your life easier, so if it's making it harder, definitely switch something up to help yourself out.

Another big positive to having a routine is that it will make it easier for you to adapt when things come up that you weren't expecting to deal with. With a preset schedule, you are capable of moving things around or switching things up do deal with certain situations.

Sometimes it takes a while to get used to having a set technique if you're not used to it. It will feel forced at first, but after a few days or weeks, it will feel so normal that you won't know what to do without it!

When people first start out trying to create a functioning routine, they often struggle and succumb to the easy way out. They just give up on trying to make their life simpler, and in turn, they make their life harder by not setting some guidelines to follow.

Of course you are going to have to make some decisions in life. That's inevitable. But, having a daily routine will make those decisions for you so much simpler.

Typically, routines can make or break you. Well-thought-out routines that fit your life's wants and needs tend to work very well and allow you to accomplish so much more in every day.

> You will be motivated to do well and seek to do well in all that you do.

You will work better and get so much more done. It will almost seem like someone is running around doing everything for you while you sit back and enjoy the independent functioning. In reality, you are getting everything done for yourself, which will give you a sense of pride and accomplishment.

You will be motivated to do well and seek to do well in all that you do. You will see that when you have a routine that you feel good about, you will want to feel good about doing everything else in your life as well. So, it just makes sense that you become more productive with a routine.

Yet again, it is so important to have that positive mindset so you can be your most productive and efficient self! Routine isn't just about writing down things that you have to do. Routine is also creating daily habits you can do that will allow you to be more successful.

Use that positive mindset that you now have to build yourself up and do some great things.

Fast Action Step:

Post a picture of your favorite daily activity with the hashtag #SurviveAndThrive. Search the hashtag to see what others are doing to enhance their days.

Organize and Prioritize

"Decide what you want, decide what you are willing to exchange for it. Establish your priorities and go to work." ~ H. L. Hunt

I have a "type A" personality, which means that I find satisfaction in getting things done. Every day, I love to make to-do lists. I grab some sticky notes, write down what I want to get done, and put them in my organizer. Throughout the day I cross things off that I finish, and I typically get everything done that I wanted or needed to. If I didn't finish (I'm not superwoman, and I certainly can't freeze time), I would make sure to write it down in my planner to complete at a later time.

My "best friend" in high school has to be my planner. My planner has literally been with me through everything. From reminding me of what to do for biology homework to seeing schedule for all of my summer softball tournaments, we've been together through it all.

Having a planner saved my life in high school. It allowed me to make the most out of my time. I was involved with three sports and countless extracurriculars, so I had very little free time. I could not afford to be stressed and worried about what I needed to do. I had to focus on maintaining my good grades, doing well in sports, and being productive in my clubs. With the help of an organizer, I could create a schedule that allowed me to fit all of that in and more.

I also use a calendar on my cell phone which comes in handy as well since we always have our phones attached to our hips. It's so simple to just open up the app or your organizer and write in what you will be doing.

My biggest hindrance is procrastination. I absolutely hate that word. I don't ever want to be characterized by it. I have learned in my high school career that the more I procrastinate, the harder it is to finish my work and get good grades. When a teacher assigns something in my class, I try to complete it as soon as possible. Pushing back my work makes me feel stressed out, and it inevitably gives me a bigger workload than what it should have been. When that happens, I want to kick myself for not completing my assignments sooner.

Students fail to prioritize and organize their lives in high school because of lack of effort. It is so easy to fall behind in high school, and if you don't keep up, you can begin to let yourself fall into a never-ending black hole where you don't get any work done. It will seem like you will never be able to catch back up to where you once were. All of those overdue math homework sets start piling up night after night, and you start to lose your grip on everything in life.

In order to pass high school, all you really have to do is complete your assignments. So when you're lazy and unmotivated, you won't do well. But when you're on top of things, you're successful. Don't be a slacker. Do your work when it's assigned and stay ahead.

Now, sometimes it can be hard to avoid some form of procrastination because of all the extra activities we're involved in. Sports practices every day, volunteer service hours, the list could go on forever depending on what your involvements and commitments. Your time gets sucked away so quickly and your to-do list becomes overwhelming. So here's my mastered game plan for kicking high school's butt.

You can use your planner in so many ways. You can record everything you need to do monthly, weekly, and/or daily--thus organizing and prioritizing your life! Having things written down makes it so much easier to remember what you need to finish, and you will find yourself completing everything that you need to because you can physically see it.

Here, you are organizing your life in a way that makes sense to you. You can check off things that you complete throughout the day- giving you a sense of accomplishment and better organizational skills.

This also allows you to have much better time management skills. Once you've settled into a routine, you save a lot of time and get more done. Then once you've organized your to-do lists and prioritized your activities, you will save even more time. Everything will be in order, and you can run through things with ease.

Prioritizing comes after organizing. First you get everything that you must do in line, then you can prioritize and decide what is most important and what's least important. Take on things that have a closer due date and projects that require a lot of work. Then the less difficult tasks can be acted upon later, after the prior assignments have been fully completed.

It makes it harder to stick with prioritizing when you start something, then start another thing, and another. That cycle does not help you to be successful in any manner. Once you start a task, try your best to finish it. You won't have all of these half-finished projects that need your immediate attention. Do the things of greater importance first, then tackle the ones of lesser importance. It's easier to focus on one thing at a time. This will make you so much more efficient in the way you work. You will feel in control of your life and more powerful than ever.

> You will feel in control of your life and more powerful than ever.

When you're organized and everything is prioritized, you will live with a sense of purpose. You know exactly what needs to be done, when to do it, and how to do it. You can start to think more creatively and make fewer mistakes.

Soon you will be excelling in all of your classes and be one step closer to rocking your high school career.

Fast Action Step:

Post a picture of your organizer or schedule with the hashtag #SurviveAndThrive. Search the hashtag and encourage someone else on their journey to survive and thrive.

Relationships

"How people treat you is their karma; how you react is yours." ~ Wayne Dyer

During my high school journey, I have built lasting relationships that will benefit me well into my future endeavors. My freshman year I was introduced to some amazing people. I found role models within my school and community who were willing to help me do well in everything that I did.

I knew that when I entered high school, I wanted to make a positive impression. I wanted people to view me as a beacon of light- someone who had the strength and ability to start a movement and change things for the better. Looking back, I know that I did just that. Once again, it all started with the mindset

> I envisioned my goal, and I achieved it.

that I gave myself. I envisioned my goal, and I achieved it.

I have had the honor to represent several organizations and teams during my four years. Every year I have been the captain of the softball team, which enabled me to really show my leadership early on as a freshman. I gained people's respect and trust. People knew that they could count on me when they needed to.

Because of my success on the softball field, people started reaching out to me in other areas of my life. Soon, it wasn't just that I wanted to be a leader; everyone around me wanted my influence as well. I was elected as President of the National Honor Society and class secretary. My classmates would come to me for advice, looking for answers to their questions. When anyone needed a helping hand, I made sure that mine was outstretched. And the aftermath of that--I had an abundant number of outstretched hands in return.

Any time that I needed help, there were more than enough people willing to help me with whatever I needed. I am ever so grateful for that because I understand that it takes a lot of personal effort to assist others.

Recently, I had a sophomore approach me about running for the president's position for the National Honor Society since there would be a vacancy, seeing that I am approaching graduation. I had been involved with this student before because of our extracurricular activities and sports, and because of the impression that she first gave me, I jumped on the opportunity to help her.

After I expressed my support of her, I had a realization. She had come to me because she trusted me. I had established a relationship with her that was honorable.

I appreciate the fact that my classmates and peers are inclined to come to me in their time of needs. They need someone who's credible, and I certainly have identified myself as a credible individual.

I have had so many opportunities to associate with other people who were involved in the same things that I was; I just didn't know they were there. This boosted me up and propelled me to go farther in my activities and life in general. I had a platform of people who were there to help get me places. They knew what it took to climb to the top of the ladder, and because of the gracious relationship I had founded with them, they surely used all of their power to get me to the top as well.

We make impressions on people within seconds of actually meeting them. Having sound relationships during your high school career will certainly set you up for forthcoming victory. Without the guidance of others, we are literally left all on our own. It is so overwhelming to do everything by yourself. You need partners, teachers, and coaches. Before you know it you will have a whole cheering squad to share your entire life with!

If you have a group of people who are eager to encourage you, things will come to you with ease. In the end, your selfless assistance will come back twofold. So do it now. One more thing that you will thank yourself for later.

Networking with others can take you so far in life. The networking part of relationships is really where we become profitable. When you've established solid relationships with others, you have a bond. When you're on good terms, you can use those relationships as notable tools. The people that you know and stand with on good terms can significantly help you to make further connections with people that they know. That's called networking. You meet someone new through a mutual friend. It's a novel relationship for the both of you, but it's a resourceful connection.

For example, when applying for colleges, your networks can give you awesome recommendations. Your connections can help you get that job that you really want. The people who you have founded valuable relationships with can really take you far in life. You will see that you can get everything that you want and more as long as you have surrounded yourself with the right people.

You get out of friendships what you put in. You need to show people that you're courteous, thoughtful, and well-mannered. Once people see that maturity instilled within you, they will be more inclined to hop on board your train. You form that mutual respect for one another and go on to do wonderful things from there.

Be observant during your interactions. If you notice that someone seems particularly interested in you and your abilities, show them that interest right back. Get to know them and see if you can help one another out. If you can, that's great! Take what you have and run with it.

Do what's best for you and the lives around you. Work hard to make a positive impact with your loved ones and friends. Get with the people who want to encourage you. Those are the people who see your true potential and will get you to the top. Find some good-hearted, like-minded individuals and watch your life begin to blossom!

If the person that you are trying to have a friendship with isn't putting forth as much effort as you are, then don't let yourself suffer. When you don't see some common interests between the two of you, then it's okay to let this contact go. It's not healthy to keep chasing and pushing people to get what you want. If they're not initially willing to be a part of your life, then things aren't worth your precious time and effort.

You cannot keep going through the motions. That's like taking one step forward and two steps back. You really aren't getting anywhere with those people. Now is the time to shape up your life. Trim off the fat. Get rid of the people who aren't supporting you and your goals.

Fast Action Step:

Post a picture of you and a family member or friend and use the hashtag #SurviveAndThrive. Search the hashtag to see how others are connecting with their loved ones.

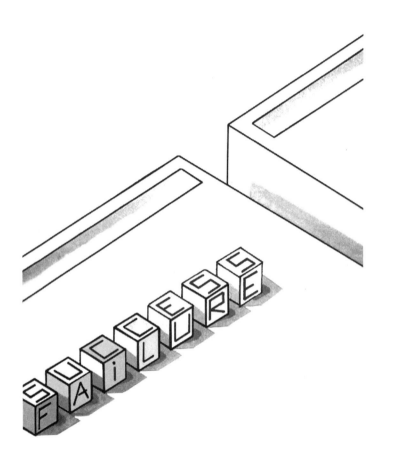

Failure and Confidence

"With confidence, you have won before you have started." ~ Marcus Garvey

All of my life, everyone said that I was so perfect. I never did anything wrong, and nothing bad ever happened to me. All I can say to that is wow--that could not have been further from the truth!

I have worked so hard for everything that I've accomplished. I have poured all of my heart, time, and soul into my goals, and things have turned out pretty fantastic. I see now that with the right amount of energy and determination, anything is possible.

I was also very lucky. I did not really have to face my personal failure until late in my high school career. I had applied to get into a university's honors college. Unfortunately, I was not accepted. I didn't make the cut.

Of course, I was devastated after I found out that they didn't want me. This is something that I had worked so hard in school for! I always set my sights high with my grades and aimed to be at the top of my class. I did great with all of my sports and clubs; I thought I was totally ready to be entered into this honors program. Obviously the college thought otherwise--which has turned out to be a great thing for me.

I was not used to dealing with failure. In the past, I had worked my hardest for things that I wanted, and in return, I got what I wanted! My work ethic was stellar. But then, I got that bad news. If I hadn't been equipped to deal with the situation properly, I might have really let the rejection get to me.

I decided from the time I applied (because I knew that they would either accept me or reject me) that I would be proactive. So I began to prepare for the best possible scenario and the worst.

I prepared for the honors college to accept me. I researched what I would get to do if I got in. I looked at the classes I would be taking and the people I would be working with.

It was satisfying for me to learn that no matter what, whether I got into the honors program or not, the university would challenge me regardless. I was still earning my college degree with all of the same credentials and opportunities. The only difference seemed to be the class sizes. With the honors courses, classes were smaller. But it's good for me because this will help me to learn how to stand out in a crowd and get myself noticed.

I prepped myself to be denied from the program by finding all of the other opportunities that the university still had to offer me. If I got rejected, I would already know that it wouldn't be the end of the world. There were still SO many things out there for me to do and do well with! There is no stopping me!

Failure is inevitable. It's a part of life that eventually we all must face. Some of us will face failure early on as children, some in middle school, some in high school, and some in college. Sooner or later we are all going to fail at something.

Take failure as a compliment, a lesson. Look for it in everything! Once you find your lessons, you will begin to learn so much more about life, and failure will come less and less often.

But when the missteps come, we must be prepared to deal with them. The solution is confidence. My situation I spoke of earlier blends in with self-confidence. If I didn't allow myself to exhibit so much self-

> The solution is confidence.

confidence, I *know* that I would not have even applied to the honors college in the first place!

Confidence is the key to success. Without it, would we ever muster up enough courage to step out of our comfort zone to try new things and reach for our goals? Probably not.

Once you learn to love yourself for who you are, the confidence will come.

Confidence boosts your self-esteem. It lets you stand up for yourself and your beliefs. It lets you say no when you're overwhelmed. It lets you tackle unfamiliar yet intriguing tasks.

Self-confidence will take you anywhere you want to go. Start to believe in yourself and what you're capable of.

No one can force you to feel confident about yourself; only you can. Sure, they can tell you things that will make you feel good and want to keep striving for the best, but ultimately, it's you who decides whether or not you love who you are or hate who you are.

Let me repeat myself one last time: you need to start living your best life now by making decisions for yourself, picking your mindset, setting a routine, organizing your life, creating lasting relationships, preparing to deal with failure, and deciding that you love your life.

Decide that you are living the best life that you possibly could, and if you can't say that you love yourself, change something. Go back and reevaluate everything, find the flaw, and fix it!

Do things you love. Surround yourself with people you love and who love you. Give your best effort with everything. Take every chance you get. Regret nothing. Look at the bright side. See the good in every day and everyone. Live true to your values and morals.

And most importantly, *never* give up. Shoot for the moon. The sky is the limit and you can do anything, absolutely anything, that you set your mind to. It's never too late. If you're in high school, it is the perfect time to start building up your portfolio and reputation. Get ahead of the game now, and life will be so much easier in the years to come.

I promise that remarkable things will start to come to you.

Fast Action Step:

Post your absolute favorite picture of something you love with the hashtag #SurviveAndThrive. Search the hashtag to see what other things people love who are surviving and thriving.

Special Thanks

Thank you to Alycia Darby for inspiring and directing me from beginning to end of this book. Your advice and countless hours of instructions were tremendously helpful. You made this possible!

Thank you to Mrs. Kami Oldham for helping and researching with me. Your guidance was so appreciative, and of course, your joyful attitude was encouraging as well.

Thank you to Mrs. Melissa McDonald for being my second mother in high school. During some weeks, it felt as if I saw you more than I did my actual mother. Your support, encouragement, and dedication will never go unrecognized.

Contact the Author

For bookings and praise, please contact the author at:
About.me/Emaleigh.Mowry